THE LITTLE BOOK OF Good Enough

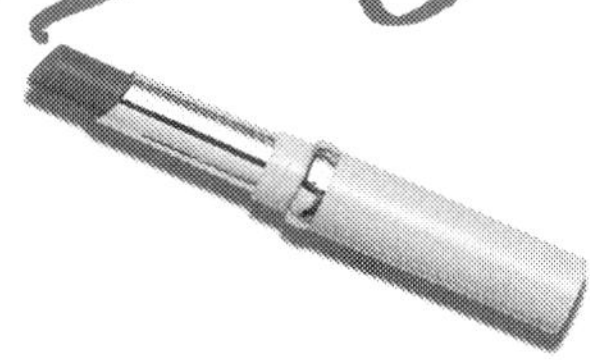

Quiet Your Inner Critic, Ditch The Doubt, And Own Your Worth

EIMEAR ZONE

Publishing Services provided by Paper Raven Books

Printed in the United States of America

First Printing, 2018

Paperback ISBN= 978-1-7327158-0-6
Hardback ISBN= 978-1-7327158-1-3

For my daughter, Aerin
and my dear friends
Ruth, Karen, Charlotte, Jannet, and Nia

Table Of Contents

You can find additional free resources to accompany this book, including exercise worksheets, on the author's website **www.eimearzone.com**

Introduction

I'm not sure when it started exactly, but I got the message quite early on. Girls shouldn't be too loud or boisterous. Girls should be polite and accommodating. Girls should be thin and pretty. A cuss word sounds worse when it comes from a girl rather than a boy. On and on it went! I even remember being told by my mother that a man should be able to circle his hands around a woman's waist! I'm not sure what happened to women who couldn't meet that standard, but I got the impression that it definitely wasn't good. Considering my childhood nickname was "Fatty," this was particularly troubling news. It seemed to me that girls just weren't supposed to take up much space in the world.

The thing is that doesn't work for me—not at all! I think it's time for girls and women to take up a lot more space in the world, in every arena.

Change is coming, albeit slowly. In my lifetime, laws and social norms have changed. There are obstacles still, though, and discrimination and bias most definitely persist. But beyond these factors, is there something else at play? Is there something else stopping women from taking up more space? When the society you live in wasn't built by you or for you but by those who didn't necessarily envision you taking up a lot of space within it, can this hold a girl back?

I think it can and does and it manifests in thoughts and feelings of not being enough.

The truth is that from the moment you drew your very first breath, you were enough. When you woke up this morning, you were enough. Many of us struggle with accepting this fact, that we are inherently worthy, inherently "good enough." Instead, we find ourselves in a seemingly unending battle with an inner critic, constantly questioning our own competence, our own value, and ultimately our worth. Too often this inner critic will rob us of many of the potential treasures and the joy life has to offer as we respond by hesitating, stepping back from opportunities, and ultimately retreating into smaller lives.

The Little Book of Good Enough is a tool to tame that inner critic, to reclaim and boost your self-worth, and to set you on the path to the life you truly deserve: a life of opportunities grasped and dreams pursued—a life lived without regret.

Well, OK, that all sounds great, Eimear, but how do I get that off the page and into my head and live like I truly believe it?

I'm so glad you asked! Because this book is a tool to do just that. Yes, it will take work. It isn't enough to go on Pinterest and dive into a sea of positive thinking quotes. You'll actually have to unpack some of your long-held beliefs and behaviors, employ some targeted self-awareness, and yes, get uncomfortable. Or, you could just go back to scrolling through your social media feed and trying to manage all those waves of self-doubt, which at times may even escalate to self-loathing…

Nah! You've been there. Let me show you a way forward instead.

Who Have You Let in Your Head?

Let's begin by getting clear on one important thing. It should seem obvious, but it absolutely bears repeating.

Our worth, yours and mine, has nothing to do with:

- How much we earn
- How prestigious our job is, if we have one
- The college we attended, or didn't
- How thin or fat we are
- The type of home we live in
- How fit or not we are
- How pretty we are
- Whether we drive a Tesla or take the bus
- Whether we're single or in a relationship

I could go on, but I know that you're absolutely amazing and smart, and I'm certain that you've worked out where I'm going with this. These things merely describe your life situation. They are not you, and they are not your worth.

I'm sure that if I asked you whose opinion you valued, that you could quite easily give me the names of those people. It would probably be quite a short list. These are, naturally, people you are close to, confide in, and respect. What I'm less sure of is whether you actually listen to these people.

Now, how about strangers or acquaintances? Do you ever imagine or even assume that other people are judging you, and that their opinion might not be altogether flattering? I call this "FOWOT" as in, **F**ear **O**f **W**hat **O**thers **T**hink. Don't get me wrong, having an active imagination is an extremely valuable asset, when it is used for problem solving or in any other creative pursuit, but not when it's used like this. This isn't positive creativity, this is the rocket fuel of crippling negativity and self-doubt where we risk descending into the jungle of "What if…?"

What if I try and I screw up and fall flat on my face…
What if they think I'm arrogant…
What if it doesn't work out, and I have to retreat to my old life…
What if they're thinking, "Who does she think she is?"

We all have our own version of this script, and it's important to bring it into the light of our consciousness. Sometimes we may experience it at a more subliminal level, if it's lived with us for a long time. We might just have a deep sense of unease or anxiety and not actually explore beyond that. However, the results will be the same whether we're conscious of our particular "What If" script or not; we'll withdraw, go small, and play safe. But right now, we're going to expose and explore it. It hates to be brought into the light for a very good reason, because, on close examination, it looks totally ridiculous! Also, when we bring it out from the shadows and into the light, it loses a lot of its power. But, one step at a time.

Exercise 1

Take a moment and let's unburden you of some FOWOT. Consider what fears, what "what ifs" might be affecting you, manifesting as FOWOT. Don't overthink this or worry about getting it right or perfect. If you find it difficult to begin, just start to freewrite—write whatever comes to mind—as you look at the title below.

You can either fill in your thoughts on the sheet below or in a separate notebook, if you prefer. Begin now, and don't get up from your seat until you're done. If you feel uncomfortable, acknowledge it, but do keep going anyway.

I FEAR OTHERS MIGHT THINK THAT…

Congratulations on getting something down on paper! Many people never explore these inner fears and just drift along forever under their influence and never challenge them. You are clearly not one of those people. You have decided to steer your own ship.

Now, my question is, FOR WHAT is all this FOWOTing? Let's drop our first Truth Bomb!

Truth Bomb #1

Most of the planet is, in fact, not thinking about you—like, at all! They are literally completely caught up in their own stuff.

This isn't meant as an insult, I assure you, but rather as a friendly nudge to remind you not to waste energy worrying about what other people might think of you, or what you're doing or not doing. You are the central character in your life. I can assure you most people are too wrapped up in their own lives to be thinking of, or judging, you and yours.

Affirmation Of Worth

I am enough.
I am whole and worthy, and the sole author of my life story.

Check Your Filter!

No, I'm not talking about a smartphone filter, I'm talking about how we experience reality. I know—heavy, right?! But bear with me, I'm dropping another Truth Bomb.

Truth Bomb #2

People filter and interpret what others say or do through the lens of their *own* self-worth.

So, imagine that person in your office, at the school gate as you drop off your kids, in line at the grocery store, or maybe sitting opposite you in Starbucks. Imagine they actually look up from their smartphone for a millisecond to momentarily detach from their own preoccupations. Maybe they engage with you or hey, maybe they just look at you sideways. What do you do? Well, that all depends. How robust is your sense of self-worth in that moment?

If you're struggling in that moment, you may well imbue their innocuous words or actions with a heap of meaning that, chances are, just isn't there. We can literally make stuff up. There's that misuse of our imaginations again! Do we make good stuff up? No. No, we most definitely do not.

I remember one time when my kids were in elementary school, and I was walking out of the school gate after dropping them off. I ran into an acquaintance—a lady I knew just to say hello to in the mornings. She looked a little weary, so I asked her how she was doing. Her response? "I'm so sick of how rude and unfriendly some of the parents are at this school. They look down on me!" *Holy crap!* I thought, almost wishing I hadn't asked. She caught me on a good day, though, so instead of grimacing slightly and wishing her a "nice day," I said, "You know what, maybe whoever was rude to you today was just having a bad day—nothing more. We all have bad days, right?" She looked at me, her face softened a little as she nodded, and we said goodbye to each other.

The lens matters, and we need to be very aware of it. We filter and interpret what we see through it, and if we're feeling weary and our sense of self-worth is low, we're going to have more and more unpleasant experiences, like my acquaintance from the school gate that day. She isn't unique. I definitely saw myself in her, which is why I could empathize. I was, and still am at times, totally capable of interpreting events through that not good enough, low self-worth lens. I'm more awake to it now, though. I notice that my lens is skewed, off somehow, sooner, so I can react quicker. How do we do that though—how do we stop walking around as though we were asleep and powerless? It starts by raising our awareness. Here's what's happening right now if your sense of self-worth is low and in the absence of this awareness:

THE 5-STEP SELF-SABOTAGE SPIRAL

1. Someone says something, you see something, or something happens;
2. Your internal operating system, without much reflection or objectivity, automatically filters it through the lens of your self-worth;
3. Emotional autopilot initiates a pre-programed pattern of thoughts, feelings, and behaviors that all feed off each other;
4. Result = You feel like shit;
5. Feeling like shit sets the tone, so you repeat and reinforce 1 through 4 indefinitely.

A little oversimplified? Maybe, but only maybe.

TRUTH BOMB #3

The most effective strategy to hold on to any problem is to define it as really difficult to solve or, better yet, insurmountable.

When we repeat and reinforce a pattern so many times, it's no wonder that it can seem insurmountable. Hopefully, though, just by reading the 5-Step Self-Sabotage Spiral, your awareness is raised, and you're feeling a little more alert to the process. Fortunately, there are some helpful signposts that you can look out for, which, with practice and over time, you will begin to see earlier and earlier. Here are just a few of the more obvious. They may overlap a little, but I feel it's helpful to recognize them in as many forms as possible.

I should…:
Beware of should-ing all over yourself. When "should" turns from a suggestion into a weapon to beat yourself up with, it's a red flag.

Absolutism:
I'm *never* going to…. I *always* screw up….

Name-calling:
I'm a slob. I'm such a loser!
Would you say that to a friend—one you hope to keep?

Jumping to Conclusions:
Going from A to Z without passing literally *any* of the other letters in the alphabet!

Negative Obsessions:
You can't see beyond the worst-case scenario and are totally focused on the negative.

Catastrophizing:
One small thing goes wrong, you make one mistake, and magnify it into an outright catastrophe projecting it rippling forward into every other area of your life.

When you're triggered in this way, it could sound something like this inside your head:

"I knew I wouldn't get that promotion. I'm surprised they haven't fired me already. It's just a matter of time before they find out that I'm a complete idiot and don't have a clue what I'm doing."

"I'm such a loser. I can't seem to stop eating shit, and I'm just getting fatter and fatter, and I can't fit into anything and…"

"I'm never going to be happy. Everyone I know is getting married and having kids, and I haven't even had a real date in months, and who'd be interested in me anyway? I'm not pretty or interesting or..."

"Oh my God, my boss wants to see me about the project. She must be unhappy with my work. I knew it. I should never have taken this job. I'm not good enough."

"Shit! I totally forgot about the kids' dental appointments today! I'm just such a crap parent. I'm always screwing up."

YAWN!

I'm bored of the trash talk, aren't you? I mean, it's been hanging out for years and years, and it's never had a damn good thing to say to you, about you. It's taking up very valuable emotional real estate in that amazing head of yours.

If another person spoke this kind of trash to you, what would you do?

Exactly! You would kick their ass!

(Not advocating violence here, obviously! And I know you're smart enough to know that, but I'm just paranoid enough to write it anyway!)

Want to take out the trash? I thought so!

Affirmation Of Worth

I am enough.
I am more than the sum of my weaknesses and failures.
I am valuable and capable, and if I stumble on my path, I will rise again.

Take Out the Trash—Let In the Light

Let's step into this with a little exercise. We are going to build you up. Well, actually, you are going to do it yourself, with a little help from your friends.

Everyone, at some point in their life, has been given a compliment. Everyone! The thing is, we tend to be rather careless with these valuable nuggets. We might just glance at them before we toss them aside, and we forget to file them away properly. The bad stuff—the criticisms, the perceived slights? Oh, those dear friends! We know exactly where they are. They are kept at hand at all times as they are consulted so frequently. We have examined them under a microscope before embellishing and magnifying them.

How messed up is that?

Very messed up is what!

We're going to fix that right now. Are you in? Good!

I want you to fill out the list below. This is your Compliments List, or Damn, I'm Fabulous List, if you're feeling braver. This may well be the first time you've ever written one of these, and there's no right or wrong way to do it. I've given you space for eight but, *puhleeze*, feel free to just go for it, and as you start to uncover more and more, don't risk burying those nuggets again—capture them on paper. As before, if you prefer to do this work in your notebook, go ahead.

It may be a slow start as you overcome your internal resistance, but I want you to begin and not move from your seat until you have at least eight. What nice things have ever been said to you, about who you are, things you've done, or kind words you've said—anything positive! Write it down, and don't you dare let any feelings of being self-conscious and humble or undeserving lead you to ignore or play down your fabulousness. This is for your eyes only remember. No FOWOT allowed. Go for it!

Exercise 2

MY COMPLIMENTS/DAMN, I'M FABULOUS LIST

Yay! Go you! That list is you, and you've been ignoring it. That stops right now. Maybe you're not immediately ready to own it fully, and that's OK. This is your starting point. This is where that begins to change. Keep your list, re-read it often, especially at times when you feel uncertain, fearful, or not enough. And going forward from today, add to it often. Don't let any new nuggets be lost. Accept them graciously. They are yours.

Affirmation Of Worth

I am enough.
I am a beautifully complex, valuable, and talented human being.
I am completely deserving of a rich and abundant life.

Those Pesky Limiting Beliefs

We've only touched on this lightly so far—that voice in your head. Underneath and enmeshed in all of our "not good enough" self-talk is a collection of limiting beliefs. We've elevated and endowed these beliefs with fact status. Yep, that little throwaway (OK, maybe mildly insulting) comment someone made to you years ago has been elevated to the status of an ironclad truth.

Crap! Why the hell do we do that?! Well, here's what came up for me and maybe it resonates.

Because it's easier and safer to live small. It's safer to believe that you "aren't" and therefore "can't" because then you never have to try (Yippee!). And, obviously if you never try, then you'll never fail, and then you'll be saved from the humiliation that would, let's face it, inevitably follow such a reckless move (Oh, thank God! What a relief!). All those people pointing and laughing at you as they say, "Oh My God, who did she *think she was to even try that?! What a joke!"*

- A PAUSE FOR THOUGHT -

Why do we do this to ourselves and others? Why does it feel safer to judge and separate ourselves rather than to encourage our fellow women, to be their cheerleader, to forge compassionate open-hearted connection?

Maybe, just maybe, if we learned to own and celebrate our own value, worth, and potential, we would learn to see, celebrate, and elevate it in our fellow women, too.

I think we all might absolutely love that world, and only we can create it.

So, is that how you really feel? Are these limiting beliefs really a cause for celebration, a source of relief? I don't think so. No, actually, screw that!

Time to dismantle that bullshit, and it will take you getting uncomfortable. Listen, being "comfortable" hasn't served you very well. "Comfortable" hasn't brought you fulfillment. Everything new, every move forward and up to more, always brings discomfort, initially. That's what growth feels like. You're here because you want a change, because you want to let go of "not good enough" and to transform. So, onward! Let's dive into the next exercise.

Exercise 3

You're going to write a list of five to eight beliefs that you hold about yourself. These are the beliefs that you keep in deep storage, locked in the dark corners hidden from view, which you desperately try to ignore, run from, and deny. Yep, I know, this is panic-inducing stuff! But, you know what? Those little buggers are running the show right now and ruining stuff for you. They rob you every single day. They keep you scared and small when you should be reaching out and up and taking up more and more space in this beautiful world. So, it's time to take them out and bravely look at them in the cold light of day.

I've been here, and I'm going to help you get off the starting block with some of my own examples from this work:

I believe that I am merely average with no noteworthy strengths.

I believe that I am weak and lack the discipline to achieve and progress.

See! Yes, writing that made me feel pretty vulnerable and queasy, but it feels great to be on the other side of it. You can do this! Start writing, and don't leave your seat until you're done. Deep breath. You are worthy and deserving of this work. Begin!

THE SHITTY LITTLE BELIEFS I'VE DEVELOPED ABOUT MYSELF

Well done! Big exhale! It can feel really overwhelming to look deeply within ourselves and to acknowledge these things. I'm hugely proud of you, because that is tough work, and you just did it. These beliefs that you've been carrying around are so, so heavy, and they don't serve you.

Now, let's reality-check some of these Shitty Little ("SL") Beliefs, shall we? On page 24, or in your notebook if you prefer, choose three to four of the beliefs you wrote down and think of just one single example of why that belief is not a fact, why it simply is not true.

I'll get you off the starting block again with an example, because I know when I did this, I found it so challenging and uncomfortable! I spent ages looking at the paper, thinking:

This whole process is BS! All these beliefs are true, obviously, or else it wouldn't take me this bloody long to think of just one example to disprove them!

Yep, it wasn't a smooth process but more akin to a toddler tantrum. This example is from a time when I did this work for myself.

Example:

OLD SL BELIEF

I'm too old/I've been out of the workforce for too long to start a new venture.

JUST ONE EXAMPLE OF WHY IT'S BULLSHIT

There are plenty of people who have begun successful businesses after the age of 40. [Once you get that one thing, you'll want to say more!] I'm passionate about my purpose, and I'm a hungry learner. I've kept up with the business world and my niche, and I'm tech- and social media savvy. I've been constantly learning and upskilling over the years and I have so much to offer.

NEW SPARKLY EMPOWERING BELIEF

I am a vibrant being growing into my fullest self. I learn and improve daily and I have an abundance of wisdom and talent to contribute.

OK. You can't put this off any longer. Remember, stay at this and don't leave your seat until you're done. Yes, it is uncomfortable and YES YOU CAN do this. Breathe. Go!

Exercise 4

Woo-hoo! You did it! I knew you could, and you did. Congratulate yourself. You have come a long way. Lots of people can't bring themselves to end the self-deception and to get truthful with themselves. They prefer to continue the deception and live the small unexamined life, masked in busy. But that's not for you. You've taken a big step forward. Breathe in the rare air as you unshackle yourself.

But we've got more to do.

Affirmation Of Worth

I am enough.
I am strong and I do not let my fears control me.
I choose to look them in the eye, challenge, and move beyond them.

Friend or Foe

Have you ever asked yourself, "How did I get here?!" when you're feeling frustrated with a situation you find yourself in, be it in your professional life, a personal relationship, or your home situation? Well, let me drop another Truth Bomb on you.

Truth Bomb #4

We are always creating the reality that we are most committed to having.

Let that sink in for a minute before you go on a "WTF?!" rant. You say you want to do, achieve, be, have certain things, or stop behaving in certain ways, but it just never seems to pan out. You find yourself in a looped experience. It all starts off well, but you find yourself falling away from your original plan. You might have heard people describe this as "self-sabotage." What's all that about?

Let's use another exercise to take a look.

Exercise 5

First of all, can you think of any goal or desire you've had for a long time that you just can't seem to realize? It can be something from any area of your life. Write it here.

MY JUST-CAN'T-SEEM-TO-MAKE-IT-HAPPEN GOAL

Example: I want to get fit enough to run a half marathon.

Now—and here you need to get curious, open-minded, and imaginative—detach a little and consider what underlying commitment someone might have made to themselves to prevent them from reaching this goal. Re-read that last sentence and digest it. What fear-based promise could they have made to themselves, that they wouldn't openly or consciously acknowledge, that could explain why they haven't managed to reach this goal?

Possible Underlying Commitments/Fear-Based Promises I've Made:

- I'm committed to struggling with my fitness because that means I can expend a huge amount of time and energy on the process and thereby have an excuse to avoid doing other things that scare me more.

- I'm committed to not getting fit, because my closest friends all struggle with their fitness, and if I achieved this, I might feel isolated from my social group.

I think this exercise is perhaps the most challenging, because it's really key to understanding what unconscious force is directing your behavior. Unless you see it, you can't take back control.

Just have a go. Let go of any pull toward perfectionism, or the need to get it "right." Just engage in honest, open-hearted, judgment-free exploration. No one gets to see this but you. Messy is fine. Just go!

POSSIBLE FEAR-BASED PROMISES/UNDERLYING COMMITMENTS I'VE MADE THAT KEEP ME FROM MY JUST-CAN'T-SEEM-TO-MAKE-IT-HAPPEN GOAL

Great work! You got something down on paper. However messy and painful it was to do, it's there. Don't worry if you're not sure if you've identified exactly what your fear-based promise/underlying commitment may be yet. It's taking off the blinkers and beginning the work of exploring that are most important at this stage. Be patient and kind with yourself. You're beginning to explore where you're undermining yourself, and that's an uncomfortable concept to confront—that you could be treating yourself as more foe than friend. Congratulations! Really, this is no small thing.

Affirmation Of Worth

I am enough.
I am brave and strong enough to move beyond my self-deception and to embrace the abundant life I deserve.

Committing To Better

I came across a Native-American story recently, and it resonated strongly with me. It goes like this. A grandfather was talking with his son about the cruelty and violence that exists in the world and how it comes about. The grandfather described it akin to two wolves fighting in his heart. One wolf, he said, is angry and vengeful and the other, kind and understanding. The grandson asked which wolf would win this fight for his heart, to which his grandfather replied, "The one that wins will be the one I choose to feed."

We have a choice. The outcome depends on our choices.

TRUTH BOMB #5

We live in the aftermath of our choices.

Some choices we're fully conscious of, but some are now so automatic that they have become our habits and our behaviors. Our outcomes though, how we experience life in essence, is down to these choices, habits, and behaviors. If we want a different outcome, we're going to have to take a closer look at the choices, habits, and behaviors that we're making today.

Exercise 6

Think now about any choices you have made, any habits and behaviors you may have that could be keeping you from your goal. Get real with yourself. Which wolf have you been feeding through your choices, habits, and behaviors? The path to freedom, the path to owning your worthiness, to feeling enough, requires you to accept yourself fully and without self-deception. You need to open your eyes and compassionately, without judgement, really look and see.

Either below or in your notebook, write as much as you feel makes sense for you. Again, don't get up from your seat until you've finished writing. Sometimes it takes sitting with the discomfort for a while, to freewrite without judgement, or it simply takes time to uncover what's going on. So, if you need to take a short break before you begin, do that now. Then dedicate this time, uninterrupted, to you. Begin.

POSSIBLE CHOICES, HABITS, OR BEHAVIORS THAT MAY BE KEEPING ME FROM MY JUST-CAN'T-SEEM-TO-MAKE-IT-HAPPEN GOAL

Another step forward and away from self-deception, another courageous action taken—congratulations! When you look at this list, what do you see? If you think about the story of the wolves, you were either feeding the wolf that represents your goal or the wolf that represents an underlying commitment, a fear-based promise to yourself. Hopefully this exercise, by taking the time to examine how you have been unconsciously placing obstacles in your own path, will help you to awaken and see with fresh eyes what has been in your way. Only when we're prepared to really look and see like this can we put ourselves in a position to change a pattern and step onto another path, a path that truly serves us and will lead us to where we long to be.

Right now, you may feel elated or you may feel pretty uncomfortable, because you've just come face-to-face with something you've been hiding and running from, maybe for years. It's OK though, don't panic! Don't run! Why? Because you know exactly where that escape path leads to already, don't you? And it's no escape. It's a well-trodden path, and God knows you've shed some tears there. Let's go somewhere else instead, shall we? It's time for fresh views and new territory. Are you in?

In the Buddhist tradition, there is a concept called *renunciation*. Renunciation basically means learning how to let go of holding on and holding back. It's realizing that these cravings we have for the safety and security of old patterns are deceptions that don't serve us, and just keep us living small lives, in fear and doubt. It's about letting go of our limiting beliefs, the ones we studiously fuel with storylines, letting go of the excuses and behaviors that don't serve us, and stepping forward.

Holy crap, that sounds scary!

It's new, so you're naturally uncertain and uncomfortable. Every time we try something new, we are extending our comfort zone, and we'll come up against a new edge as we do. There we'll pause again—or maybe, let's face it, freeze in terror—and we'll have to re-evaluate, look at this fear, acknowledge it, and endeavor to extend our comfort zone yet again. But that's life, isn't it? How much space do you think you're worthy of taking up in this world? A lot more than you're currently occupying is my guess!

How about imagining better? Now that we've had a little shuffle around inside our heads and unloosened some of the stuff we no longer want or need, it's time to think about what we truly *do* want. It's time to be purposeful and to commit to better.

Exercise 7

What new commitment could you make today to replace the old underlying one from Exercise 5? What new commitment could you make that would *truly* serve you in reaching your **JUST-CAN'T-SEEM-TO-MAKE-IT-HAPPEN GOAL?** What would you need to commit to, to make that goal your reality?

Take your time. Write down a few different options rather than limiting yourself or getting too caught up in finding a single "right" answer. Get thoughtful, creative, and engaged, and just get something down on paper. Begin.

MY SHINY NEW COMMITMENT TO ME

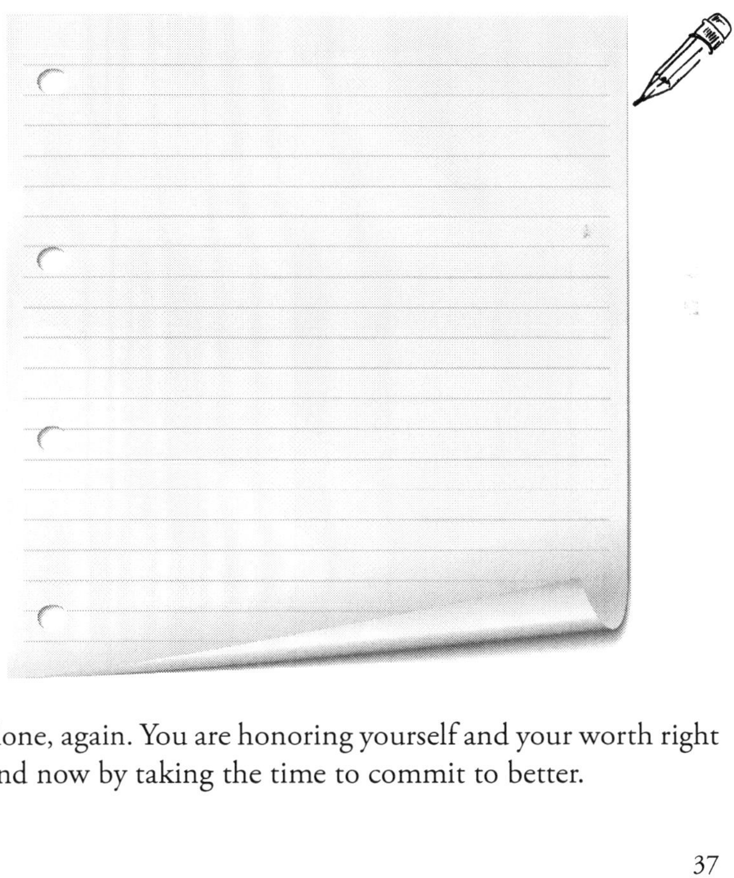

Well done, again. You are honoring yourself and your worth right here and now by taking the time to commit to better.

Affirmation Of Worth

I am enough.
Every day I move closer to the abundant life that is my birthright through my thoughts, choices, and actions.

Visualize Your Success

In a moment, I'll invite you to close your eyes, or just to rest your gaze so you're not distracted, and to imagine and visualize what your life would be like with this shiny new commitment in place. Notice how you feel and if fears begin to surface. If fears do arise, simply acknowledge the sensation but drop the storyline. Try to just be in the energy of that fear and get to know it. Be with it without turning away. If you start to run a storyline (usually prefaced with "What if…" or "I can't…"), just touch it lightly. Think of the image of a feather touching a bubble. There is no dwelling, just the lightest mental touch. Label it "thinking," and let it go.

OK, begin and take as long as you like, as long as feels right for you. If you've never done an exercise like this before, set a timer on your phone for just 10 minutes. Set one of those nice melodic tones, though, rather than something too abrupt. Begin.

Exercise 8

Now that you've spent some time visualizing where this new path will lead you, you may want to think about what resources might be useful to support your SHINY NEW COMMITMENT TO ME. For example, for the half-marathon goal, it could be getting an accountability partner, signing up for some one-on-one coaching, or downloading a running app to log your progress. The aim is to set yourself up for success. Capture any ideas and thoughts below.

RESOURCES TO SUPPORT MY SHINY NEW COMMITMENT TO ME

Perfect! These resources will provide some scaffolding to support and strengthen your Shiny New Commitment. You're taking control. You're moving forward.

Affirmation Of Worth

I am enough.
All that I need is within me.
I visualize my path and move forward, every day.

Own Your New Reality—The Magic of Mindfulness

"Be Present." We've all heard that, right? Oh, my Lord it has pissed me off, royally!

"Just breathe, and be in the moment."

WTF?! I'm busy. I'm breathing. Clearly, I am here. What more do you want from me?! Why don't I feel better yet? This isn't working! This sucks!

Let's just say, I was a little resistant to the whole mindfulness and meditation stuff at the beginning, so if that resonates with you, even a teeny-weeny bit, I get it. Stick with me though, and take a closer look at how mindful meditation could serve you. There's no chanting, and you don't even have to sit down. See? Result!

You've had a look at some of the ways you self-deceive, and now that you have, you need to work toward continued awareness. Mindfulness involves you looking at the scared little girl who wants to hold on to "not good enough," to stay small and safe, and in the same familiar loop. Mindfulness involves recognizing that you are whole, a grown-up now, and that the ingrained protective limitations you set yourself are no longer necessary. They no longer serve you. Mindfulness means powerful self-love and compassion, and letting judgment dissolve.

You need to become your own warrior in a beautiful, humor-filled, gentle, loving journey to you.

It's time to stop running away and to become your own very best friend. Let's begin.

Wherever you are, you can view your experience of this world as you occupying a sacred circle. You, of course, are the center of your circle. You can adopt the perspective that everyone and every experience that enters your sacred circle is there to teach you something. Life is about learning and growing through discovering these somethings.

You can choose to adopt an inquisitive perspective and to drop the catalog of storylines you have attached to events and people who enter your circle. The practice of mindfulness, and mindful meditation, is about learning to see the triggered storylines as early as possible, and choosing a response that nurtures and serves you, rather than allowing self-harming auto-reactions to persist.

Do you just press the mindfulness button and say goodbye forever to all those pesky unhelpful auto-reactions?

Hey, that sounds great. I'm in!

Yeah, afraid not, nope. There's no quick and dirty fix for this, and anyone who tells you differently, I would humbly suggest to you, is lying or trying to sell you something. It's a practice, it takes time, and one extremely important ingredient is self-compassion.

Example:

Say I made a Shiny New Commitment To Me in relation to the fitness goal of running a half marathon from the earlier example, which said:

I am committed to honoring my physical self through adopting and maintaining a targeted running program in order to build and maintain the strongest, healthiest, and most powerful version of me.

Now, this commitment is so new it doesn't yet have strong roots. I may have put some resources and practices in place to give it the best start possible, maybe I joined a running club or downloaded a training app and got myself an accountability buddy. But, initially, my new commitment will be fragile. Here's how you use mindfulness to help.

Into your sacred circle comes some bad news—you didn't get the promotion, your car died on the way home and your commute turned into three hours of hell…whatever. Your standard reaction is to ditch your workout plans and eat the contents of your fridge. But, you've been flexing your awareness muscle through this process, so you see that trigger. Hey, maybe you've missed your planned running session with your new club before your awareness kicks in, and that doesn't matter, it *will* kick in.

When it does, you do not need to rush and get a beautifully embroidered meditation cushion and go sit in some quiet spot and meditate. There's no chanting. It's much easier than any of that. Just pause where you are, and maybe even smile to yourself, acknowledging that you've seen the old pattern unfolding. Relax and drop the storyline that you're running to fuel the auto-reaction (the missed run in this case). There is no judgment, just some humor and self-compassion. Feel the energy devoid of the storyline. What does your body feel like? Where is there tension? Get curious just being with that energy. If the storyline tries to intrude, just touch it lightly, label it "thinking," and let it go. Remember the image of the feather touching the bubble. It's the light touch and release.

Recall or maybe re-read your commitment. Celebrate that your awareness is growing and, as a result, that you are building a future that reflects that commitment. Maybe in the example we're using, you might then choose to put on your trainers and just go for a walk. That would be a further step to giving your new commitment stronger roots. Practice, practice, practice! Your life is full of events and people who will act as triggers, so you have plenty of opportunities to practice mindfulness throughout your day, every day. And don't forget to laugh at yourself, to be kind and compassionate to yourself, and to celebrate the progress that you'll make, every single day.

The key to owning your self-worth is within you and always has been. You can't buy more self-worth no matter how wealthy you are. You can only cultivate it, within yourself, through your choices and practice. It is not conditional, but rather an absolute and irrefutable truth, our birthright. Yes, in all of our beautiful human fallibility, we make mistakes. Yes, sometimes we have doubts and find it difficult to see beyond the obstacles. Our challenges and mistakes, however, do not make us any less worthy, nor does anyone else's opinion of us. No one else gets to define our worth. It is solely, and wholly, our own.

Affirmation Of Worth

I am enough.
There will only ever be one unique amazing me in this whole world.
I am worthy of love, compassion, forgiveness, and joy, and I choose to show up for myself every single day.

In Conclusion

As this is the "Little Book" and not the "Enormous Tome" of Good Enough, I have just lightly touched on the path to increasing your sense of self-worth. There are many underlying commitments you will have made to yourself that are functioning as obstacles in your path. At times, it will seem as though the world is full of saboteurs, obstacles, and distractions. It will take time, commitment, and practice to uncover and work through them. But that's a life spent moving forward and growing rather than hiding in the shadow of self-deception and habitual patterns that only injure you and hold you back.

To own your worth is your birthright. The path to knowing you're enough is the path you're meant to take, and one that will lead you to the abundant, fulfilling, and purposeful life you so richly deserve. It's time to take up more space in this world. It's time to step out of the shadows.

I wish you every ounce of courage, strength, compassion, and self-love that you'll need to walk that path. You have all you need within you.

In loving sisterhood,

Eimear x

Just Before I Go

Many months ago, I sat at my computer, a 48-year-old woman wriggling out of her skin, looking for the next step, and I wrote this:

There is a little voice in my head

It can be very loud

It never has anything nice to say

It makes me kind of sad

I try not to listen

I distract myself for a while

I ask it to be quiet, please

I don't want to feel this bad

There is a little voice in my head

Telling me I'm not good enough

There is a little voice in my head

I'm beginning to believe what it says

We all have a little voice in our heads and, although the message may vary, the damage is the same. We fall into a feeling of not enough, unworthy. Whatever our source of fear or shame, our little voice will go there and weave a story to imprison us in a smaller life of not enough, of not *being* enough.

My journey in writing *The Little Book of Good Enough* was, for me, the antidote to the little voice in my head. She still pipes up regularly, but she's a lot quieter and is less insistent, and I'm ready for her now. I don't believe what she says. My dearest hope is that *The Little Book of Good Enough* will be of service to you and help you to tame the little voice in your head, too.

Acknowledgements

My deepest thanks to my friends Ruth O'Sullivan, Karen Smith-Beaulieu, Charlotte Harkness, Jannet Faber-Borrmann, and Nia Thomas to whom I dedicate this book. You have each, in your own way and over many years, been instrumental in my path to claiming my own self-worth. I am honored to be able to call such amazing women my friends. The sisterhood and connection we form with our female friends enrich our lives far beyond any material wealth. You are each pure treasure to me.

A particular thank-you to my friend of over 20 years, Dr. Charlotte Harkness, who read an early draft of the book and gave me valuable feedback and encouragement. Thank-you, dear friend.

I am grateful to many women and men who have written and taught on this subject, particularly Pema Chödrön, Brené Brown, His Holiness the Dalai Lama, Archbishop Desmond Tutu, Gabrielle Bernstein, and Nancy Levin. I continue to be deeply inspired and influenced by their great work.

Finally, thank-you to "Mr. Z" for your love, your support, your kindness, and your endless patience. You are my rock.

You can find additional free resources to accompany this book, including exercise worksheets, on the author's website
www.eimearzone.com

Printed in Great Britain
by Amazon

41835765R00038